Unapologetic Success

How to dream beyond your limits and unlock fulfillment in all areas of your life

By Shawniel Chamanlal

ISBN: 979-8-9898106-2-8

E-Book ISBN: 979-8-9898106-1-1

Because of the dynamic nature of the internet, any web addresses or links contained in this book may have changed since publication and may no longer be valid. The views expressed in this work are solely those of the author and do not necessarily reflect the views of the publisher, and the publisher disclaims any responsibility for them.

Printed in the United States of America

Visit:

<u>www.shawnielchamanlal.com/resources</u>
for resources to start your path of empowerment
and creating a limitless vision.

Dedication

To Dorothy Brown-Johnson,

My beloved mother, my cheerleader, and the beacon of light not only in my life but also in the hearts of those in our community. Your spirit and legacy are the cornerstones of my journey, and the essence of every dream I've dared to pursue.

You cultivated in me a confidence that has been my guiding star, encouraging me to chase my dreams with boldness and resilience. Your life, a tapestry of strength, compassion, and unwavering support, continues to inspire me and countless others.

This book, a reflection of the values and lessons you've instilled, is dedicated to you. Your legacy, Mom, lives on in every page, in every word, and in every life that finds inspiration and courage through your story.

With all my love and gratitude,
Shawniel

Table of Contents

Introduction

It's not by chance that you have come across this book. It's the beginning of a powerful transformation to courageously step into the life you've always dreamed of. It's all about building your unshakable confidence, finding a deeper sense of purpose, getting clearer on what you desire, and truly connecting with your authentic self. This is an invitation to liberate yourself from the weight of societal expectations and any self-imposed limitations in order to boldly turn your dreams into reality, and unlock fulfillment in all areas of your life.

A broken engagement in my twenties was the defining moment I felt like the universe was pressing the pause button on my life, sparking my journey to healing and self-discovery. This wasn't just a minor hiccup. It was a profound wake-up call that forced me to take a hard look at the dreams I had for my relationships, my life's purpose, and most importantly, how I saw myself.

Despite having grand visions for my future, I realized this personal setback was a clear sign that I was playing too small, settling in areas of my life where I deserved so much more, especially when it came to love.

This kick-started my transformation to align with my higher calling. It meant diving deep into changing my mindset, healing those emotional wounds that had been quietly dictating my choices, and shutting down the external noise that tried to steer my direction in life. Embracing my limitless potential wasn't just a choice. It became my mission, guiding me to experience fulfillment in ways I had only dreamed of. But let's be real, this change didn't happen overnight. It was the result of a steadfast commitment to live my truth without regrets and chase after my wildest dreams with fierce determination.

Before I met my incredible husband, I saw a pattern in my past relationships where I attracted emotionally unavailable partners. It was a cycle of frustration, dissatisfaction, and a growing distrust in connections with the opposite sex that were supposed to bring joy.

This was about the people I was choosing to entertain and a reflection of my inner state a manifestation of doubting my self-worth.

This journey of mine, filled with its ups and downs, taught me invaluable lessons about self-love, the courage to be vulnerable, and the beauty of living authentically. By facing these challenges head-on, I've been able to step into a life that's not only true to who I am, but also rich in purpose, happiness, and genuine love. It's a testament to the fact that when we dare to confront our fears and embrace our true selves, the universe has a way of aligning us with the right people and opportunities that reflect our deepest values and dreams.

Today, I stand before you as the CEO of a million-dollar practice and a respected leader in the wellness industry a position that speaks volumes of the journey I've embarked upon. At the center of my transformation was the power of visualization, emotional healing, taking actions that align with my deepest values, leaning into faith, and nurturing a community that supports and uplifts. This path I've taken has done more than just change the direction of my life. It has profoundly redefined my purpose, enabling me to empower others to chase their dreams with the same unwavering passion that has been the fuel to keep me going. My story serves as a powerful testament to the strength of resilience, the beauty of transformation, and the importance of steadfastly holding onto your vision unapologetically.

As you read this book, I want you to know that I'm not just another expert preaching what I think you should do without offering practical solutions. I have guided countless individuals, (including women leaders, entrepreneurs, CEOs, and those driven by a mission), to amplify and clarify their vision for their lives and careers, and to manifest a new life by transforming them from the inside out. I can lead you, too, not only because of my professional training and background, but because I've lived it.

This book is like having a therapist tucked away in your pocket. It's designed to guide you in creating the life you envision, encouraging you to commit to the work. Read each chapter, apply the strategies, share your journey, and embrace your unapologetic vision, knowing that you are just one choice and one change away from having the success you desire in work and in life.

With love,

Shawniel

CHAPTER 1

Dreaming Beyond Boundaries

How to Create a Limitless Vision For Your Life

Dreaming big has always been my mantra, even when those dreams seemed too vast for others to comprehend. As I navigated through the early days of my social work career, my vision was to excel within the conventional boundaries and redefine them. I envisioned myself as a wealthy social worker, an innovator and leader making global impact, writing books that change lives, and owning a thriving private practice. I believed deeply that my career in social work was a gateway to a life of abundance, challenging the traditional narrative that often confines social workers to nonprofits, community agencies, or hospital settings. When I voiced my ambition to establish a successful private practice, it was met with puzzled looks from professors and peers alike, as private practices were seen as a retirement phase and there were few examples of therapists who had ventured successfully into entrepreneurship. It felt as if I was stepping out of an assigned role, venturing into uncharted territory where a handful of therapists had dared to tread beyond conventional roles.

My aspirations seemed to defy the expected trajectory of a social worker's career, attracting doubts and limitations from those around me rather than support and encouragement. Despite being the pioneer in my family to embrace college and entrepreneurship, the skepticism I encountered only fueled my resolve. I chose to silence the chorus of doubt, focusing on crafting a vision that knew no bounds. What did it mean to be a renowned social worker? What steps were necessary to bring my dreams to fruition?

The art of scripting, a powerful visualization technique, became a cornerstone to writing the vision and making it plain. This practice involved writing down my dreams with vivid detail as if they were already my reality, going beyond mere goal-setting to mentally, physically, and spiritually preparing for my future.

Immersing myself in this narrative, I saw myself leading a successful practice, impacting lives through my books, and speaking on global stages. I envisioned a life rich in personal and professional joy, from being a present partner to my spouse and an active parent, to indulging in exotic travels around the world, truly living a life of luxury while making an impact in the field.

To amplify this vision, I employed another visualization tactic: imagining myself in an opulent restaurant where the menu limitless in its offerings was the universe itself. Here I ordered with confidence that whatever I desired be it a sumptuous New York Prime Steak, a vintage expensive wine, an international getaway, the partner of my dreams, or a fulfilling career would manifest. This practice reinforced my belief in the universe's ability to fulfill my requests, often surpassing my expectations. And it worked with my clients, too.

Cultivating Your Limitless Vision Amidst External Pressures

I want to highlight Grace, an accomplished gynecologist, who found herself wrestling with the dichotomy between her successful career and the deeper yearnings of her heart. As a Black female doctor and first-generation immigrant, she navigated a landscape riddled with microaggressions and scrutiny, where her achievements were often overshadowed by biases. The weight of her family's dreams of her becoming a prominent doctor added another layer of complexity to her aspirations, casting shadows on her true desires.

When Grace reached out to me for therapy, it was with a hope for more than just career advice. She sought a transformation that would align her life with her innermost values and unspoken dreams. Together, we ventured into the world of the limitless, where I encouraged her to envision a life untethered by her current circumstances. "What would you choose if nothing was holding you back?" This pivotal question ignited a spark within Grace, revealing her dream of leveraging her medical expertise into an entrepreneurial venture that would make healthcare accessible to communities of color, all while granting her freedom to live on her own terms.

But this life-changing decision didn't come without its fears and doubts, particularly the fear of disappointing her family and the anxiety of stepping into the unknown. Yet, Grace's longing for a life marked by purpose and joy became the compass that guided her through these challenges. She realized that to truly honor her calling, she needed to rise above familial and societal pressures.

Focusing on the joy and fulfillment her entrepreneurial dream could bring, Grace's vision for her future began to crystallize. This profound shift in perspective empowered her to make the courageous decision to leave her medical career behind and pursue her passion to start an integrative medical center. Besides this being a career change, it was a bold step toward living authentically an alliance she created with her values and aspirations.

Grace's transformation from a respected gynecologist to an innovative entrepreneur exemplifies the journey of embracing your true purpose, even when it leads you away from conventional success. Her story is woven into this chapter as a beacon of inspiration, urging you to look within and discover your own limitless vision. It's a call to action to extend yourself grace, push beyond the boundaries of external pressures, and fully embrace the life you're meant to live.

Now, it's your turn to take the limits off and begin to dream beyond any boundaries. First, list your heart's desires, understanding that everything starts with a vision, a dream, and an intention. Know that achieving the next level in your life and realizing the dream you're crafting is within reach, and that nothing is too grand for the universe to manifest. So, visualize your desires as if they're already yours.

Here's a guide to crafting your script:

- What's your strong desire?

- How does it feel to have it?

- How does it change your life?

- How does it impact those around you?

Write your responses in a present, narrative form, engaging your senses and embracing the belief that your desires have already come to pass. This will prepare you physically, mentally, and spiritually to actualize your vision. Once you've scripted your desires, immerse yourself further in the visualization exercise, feeling the joy of your achievements as if they're already part of your reality. Remember, it's not a question of if, but when.

We invite you to become a part of our vibrant community on Facebook: Unapologetic Success where you can share your limitless vision and connect with others who are just as passionate and supportive. It's a safe space designed for encouragement where every member is ready to cheer you on as you pursue your dreams. Together, in this community of dreamers and doers, we can transform our boundless potential into tangible realities.

CHAPTER 2

Navigating Success Together

"Alone we can do so little; together we can do so much." – Helen Keller

The Collective Power of Community, Mentorship, and Mindset

While becoming a wealthy and effective social worker, I yearned for a community that could resonate with and support my vision. It was near the end of graduate school that I stumbled upon a collective of social work entrepreneurs known as The Rich Social Workers. They were like-minded individuals who proved that marrying meaningful impact with financial prosperity wasn't just a pipe dream, but a tangible reality. United by shared goals, values, and aspirations, this community became my sounding board, infusing my pursuit of happiness with inspiration and motivation.

The leader of the group was a seasoned social worker turned entrepreneur who became our mentor and introduced us to a suite of training that was pivotal in sharpening the business skills essential for success. From marketing strategies to carving out a niche and mastering financial management, these sessions were instrumental in my professional growth. Our coach also challenged us to broaden our horizons by seeking out social work entrepreneurs who had trailblazed their way to success. In my research, I discovered two remarkable examples: Stacy Madison of Stacy's Pita Chips and Stedman Graham. From social work to businesswoman, Stacy showcased how the core skills of empathy, communication, and understanding human behavior could be leveraged to build a thriving business. Stacy's venture, which began with baking pita bread into chips to avoid waste, blossomed into a nationally recognized brand, eventually catching the eye of PepsiCo©. This story was a testament to the potential of social work skills in the business world, proving that it's possible to bridge one's core values with financial success.

Similarly, Stedman Graham's trajectory in his career highlighted the power of social work principles in fostering personal development, leadership, and identity. Through his company, S. Graham & Associates, he has empowered individuals and organizations worldwide to reach their full potential, emphasizing the importance of a strong sense of self a core value in social work. The inspiring stories of Stacy Madison and Stedman Graham served as real-life examples that social workers can indeed release themselves from traditional roles and achieve massive success in any field.

When we surround ourselves with examples of individuals who have transformed their visions into reality, we do more than just observe their blueprint of success. We start to see the common threads that contributed to it. This process of learning and reflecting allows us to adopt similar habits, mindsets, and strategies that are conducive to our own success. It shifts our belief system, reinforcing the idea that success is not reserved for a select few, but is accessible to all who are willing to learn and apply themselves diligently.

These success stories often highlight the importance of aligning ourselves with the right situations and people. They teach us that our environments can significantly enhance or hinder our progress. By strategically positioning ourselves in nurturing communities like The Rich Social Workers, we gain access to a network of mentorship and wisdom. This network not only cheers us on, but stretches us to grow and expand beyond our current limits.

Weaving Success Through Collective Wisdom and Empowered Communities

Empowered by the lessons learned from The Rich Social Workers community and moved by the compelling narratives of Madison and Graham, I was inspired to create a culture for growth and support within my own profession. In 2022, I founded the Abundant Therapist Collective, a vibrant community that unites therapists, coaches, and wellness professionals committed to empowering each other and cultivating the abundant lives we aspire to both personally and professionally. Understanding the significant gap in business acumen among therapists, our collective aims to be a sanctuary where we can celebrate our successes, openly address our challenges, and most importantly, have fun while focusing on wellness. This initiative is a commitment to building a nurturing network where professional advancement and personal well-being are pursued with equal passion. Experiencing community was a priceless gift that was provided to me when I needed it most, and helped to change my destiny. This opportunity to give back, to empathize and guide others on their professional journeys, is deeply fulfilling. It reflects my commitment to the progression of my peers and the continuous evolution of my own calling in social work and entrepreneurship.

In addition, I established the Unapologetic Success Community, specifically tailored to address the unique circumstances females face in leadership. Leadership, while deeply rewarding, often brings a sense of isolation, especially for women at the pinnacle of their careers. Finding peers, who celebrate our achievements as passionately as they support us during setbacks, can be rare. And in this community, you're met with professionals who not only understand, but can empathize with the distinct pressures most common to women in high positions.

At the core of the Unapologetic Success Community is the conviction that effective leadership is rooted in authenticity, purpose, and collaboration. We instill these principles in our leaders, helping to amplify and clarify their visions for both their personal lives and careers. This, in turn, fosters a transformation that reshapes them from the inside out. This process is not only about achieving professional objectives, but nurturing personal fulfillment, freedom, and well-being.

By joining this community, you're affirming your dedication to your dreams and tapping into the deep reservoir of experience, compassion, and intelligence of a community that appreciates the strength of collective ambition. The Unapologetic Success Community is here to rally behind you, offering guidance and celebrating each milestone on your path to success. Achieving unprecedented levels of success, especially when pursuing your biggest goals, requires the clarity and backing of a trusted network. The universe has an extraordinary way of connecting you with the right people at the perfect time, and sharing your aspirations with friends, coaches, or mentors can unlock doors to previously unimaginable opportunities.

As you move forward, I encourage you to dream expansively, cultivate an environment that supports those imaginations, and share your vision with those who can help bring it to fruition. Remember, no dream is too ambitious. It simply awaits your courage to take the initial step in a protective and accountable environment.

So, take a moment to pause and grab your journal. Let's delve deep into the essence of your dreams and the support system that will bring them to life. Ask yourself:

- Who are the people that make up my support team?

- What strategies and resources are essential to bridge the gap from my current reality to the realization of my dreams?

- Am I ready to fully commit and invest in the pursuit of my aspirations?

Choose at least two individuals who have achieved similar dreams, and consider what their success stories can teach you. As you journal and share your vision, remember, you are not alone. This exercise is more than a mere reflection. It is an invitation to engage, connect, and grow within a community that is rooting for your success. Your dreams are valid, achievable, and deserving of celebration. Are you ready to take that first step with us by your side?

CHAPTER 3

Living Your Truth

The Art of Cultivating a Life of No Limits

L iving unapologetically and being in tune with our desires is the essence of embracing a life of abundance. It requires a bold refusal to accept the false idea that often forces us to choose between professional success, personal freedom, and satisfying relationships. My perspective was clear from the start: compromise was not an option. I envisioned a life that transcended the typical 9-to-5 rat race. It was one that was enriched by a four-day workweek, extensive travel, joyous child-rearing, and a flourishing marriage.

This vision became clear through the creation of vision boards and the intentional use of affirmations.

These tools were not merely reflections of my deepest desires. They actively propelled me in the direction of my destiny. My vision board served as a profound mir-ror to the vision board of my soul, not only reflecting my aspirations for success, freedom, flexibility, and life's rich experiences, but revealing the shadows of doubt and fear lurking beneath.

As I gazed upon the magazine clippings and words in bold print, a rush of emotions often followed. Excitement mingled with anxiety. Hope intertwined with hesitation. The board displayed my dreams while unveiling the internal barriers in my way like the nagging impostor syndrome whispering that I wasn't enough, the ingrained belief that success was synonymous with relentless toil, and a swirling fog of uncertainties about how my dreams would come to fruition.

To confront these internal barriers, I turned to my journal, a sacred space where I could articulate and examine the feedback from my body and soul. In the silence of these early hours, journaling and prayer together provided clarity and facilitated a deep connection to my inner self. This combination has become a pivotal part of my daily practice, grounding me as I transition from the tranquility of the night into the day's possibilities. Through this practice, I learned to transform my fears into affirmations a powerful strategy for reprogramming my mindset and challenging negative beliefs. Phrases such as "I am deserving of abundance," "Success flows to me with ease," and "I am worthy of healthy relationships and a prosperous career" became my mantras. These affirmations reinforced my birthright to abundance and success and became integral in shaping the way I approached my daily activities and long-term goals.

This internal cleansing through journaling and vision boarding is proof to the power of these practices. The vision board that once highlighted my deepest fears now reflects the realization of my dreams. Today, as I step into my wellness center, I am wrapped in a heartfelt sense of peace and accomplishment. The center's serene atmosphere, enhanced by soothing melodies and the gentle cascade of water, stands as a sanctuary for healing, carrying out my initial vision of a place where counseling and holistic wellness converge a concept that once seemed far-fetched, but is now a manifestation of unwavering belief.

By journaling, vision boarding, and speaking affirmations, we harness the power of the subconscious mind, steering it in the direction of our deepest desires. The subconscious mind is like a vast repository that stores every experience, emotion, and belief we have encountered. It regulates our automatic actions and responses to the world around us, influencing everything from the way we react in stressful situations to the motivations behind our goals. Because it operates largely without our conscious input, it can often seem as though we are stuck in predetermined patterns of behavior. However, when we intentionally guide the subconscious through techniques like speaking positive statements that lift our spirits, imagining the possibilities of what can be and thinking about what we want, we can reshape our thought processes and, by extension, our life experiences. Therefore, by consistently visualizing our goals and reinforcing our belief in our ability to achieve them, we align our energy with the frequency of success, attracting opportunities and resources that bring us closer to our dreams.

From Doubt to Destiny Through Vision and Affirmation

This method has not only shaped my own journey, but also lit the way for my clients to find their paths to success. Sophie is a vibrant life coach bubbling over with dreams, yet plagued by unrelenting doubts and procrastination. Her aim wasn't to inspire on a small scale, but she envisioned herself reaching audiences far and wide, making a real difference. However, uncertainties like, *Are my dreams too big? Do I really have what it takes?* filled her mind, and Sophie found herself in a place I knew all too well. That moment of honesty, seeing her fears not as stop signs but as signposts to change her direction in life was a game-changer for Sophie.

During one session, Sophie reclined on the plush, inviting couch in my warmly decorated office, closed her eyes and took a deep, calming breath. Soft, ambient music enhanced the serene atmosphere, enveloping us in tranquility. With each breath, Sophie sank deeper into relaxation, shedding the tension that burdened her.

My voice, gentle yet firm, guided her through a body scan exercise, bringing awareness from her forehead down through her entire body. "Notice any sensations of tightness or release? I said. "Let your breath ease any tension." Attuned more deeply with each guided passing of time, Sophie's focus shifted inward, making her increasingly aware of subtle bodily sensations. This internal examination continued with Sophie exploring and acknowledging each area without judgment. She was merely observing.

As the session progressed, Sophie's breathing deepened, and her body relaxed further into the couch's soft cushion. Whenever she felt tension, I reminded her to breathe into those areas, allowing the discomfort to dissolve gradually. By the end of the body scan, she was filled with a profound sense of peace and clarity. Upon opening her eyes, the determination in her gaze was palpable. Her previous doubts diminished and were replaced by a serene wave of confidence.

Reflecting on the exercise's insights, we discussed their relevance to her aspirations. This simple screening of her inner being connected Sophie to her body's wisdom, revealing the roots of her disbelief and setting the stage for self-discovery. Through the body scan exercise, Sophie held her desires closely, believing in her ability to make them come true while attending to any arising physical or emotional responses. This wasn't only a relaxation technique, but an intimate dialogue with her body and mind, exploring underlying tensions and mental resistances.

Similar to being in a meditative state, the exercise allowed Sophie's subconscious mind to trace back to a pivotal childhood incident when a teacher's dismissive remarks sowed seeds of self-doubt. Addressing these deep-seated beliefs and finding its origin required more than just recognition. It demanded healing and reframing. Together, we delved into Sophie's history, identifying and celebrating her achievements and strengths, effectively challenging the narrative that she wasn't smart enough or capable. This process both disputed negative thoughts and built a foundation of evidence in her present day that showcased Sophie's intelligence, resilience, and worth.

Journaling became an essential tool for Sophie, enabling her to redefine her internal dialogue. "I am capable and destined for greatness" and "My voice has the power to inspire" became her mantras during moments of uncertainty. These affirmations uprooted her doubts and became declarations of her truth, boosting her belief in her potential and her right to pursue grand dreams.

Sophie going from a state of paralysis to confidently securing speaking engagements and writing her first book illustrates the power of what happens when we refuse to back down from our fears, and fearlessly take the limits off. Through self-awareness, healing, and a steadfast belief in our capabilities, we can navigate the path from dreaming to doing, turning our deepest desires into our lived experiences.

Now, I invite you to engage in this body scan exercise. Find a quiet and comfortable space where you can sit or lay down without distractions. Close your eyes and take a few deep breaths, allowing yourself to settle into the present moment.

Begin by bringing your awareness to your forehead. Notice any sensations of tension or relaxation in this area. With each inhale, imagine breathing in peace and clarity, and with each exhale, release any stress or worry you may be holding on to.

Next, move your attention down to your jaw. Notice if you're clenching your teeth or holding any tension in this area. Take a moment to consciously relax your jaw muscles, allowing them to soften and release.

Then, shift your focus to your neck and shoulders. Notice any tightness or heaviness in these muscles. With each breath, imagine sending relaxation and ease into these areas, melting away any tension with each exhale.

Continue scanning your body, moving down to your chest, your arms, your stomach, your hips, your legs, and your feet. Take note of any sensations you experience along the way, whether it's warmth, tingling, or a sense of heaviness.

When you complete the body scan, take a moment to journal and think about what you've discovered. Are there any areas of stress or discomfort that you need to pay more attention to in your daily life? Are there any emotions or thoughts that surfaced during the scan that you'd like to survey further?

Finally, take a few moments to set intentions for the day ahead. How can you carry this sense of peace and awareness with you? What affirmations can you recite to support you in facing any challenges or anxiety that may arise?

The body scan is an effective practice for cultivating self-awareness, promoting relaxation, and actively reshaping your mindset to support your journey to success. By incorporating it into your daily routine, you can begin to recondition your subconscious mind and create lasting change in your life. If you need additional support, reach out to a licensed therapist who can guide you through healing and help you to alter your belief system.

CHAPTER 4

From Vision to Reality

Take Intentional Actions to Craft Your Path and Align Spiritually

When I set out to build Healing Springs Wellness Center, I knew that it demanded an intentional action plan to map out my vision one that combined practical steps with spiritual alignment. One that wasn't just a checklist, but a roadmap intricately woven with my values, my purpose, and my unwavering commitment to making a tangible impact.

My crystal-clear vision was at the heart of this endeavor a vision not just of bricks and mortar, but of a sanctuary that fostered healing, community, and empowerment. It was expansive, encompassing the physical space and also the array of programs, workshops, and community initiatives I passionately believed in. Breaking down this grand vision into real, actionable steps was paramount.

The first step was to define the essence of Healing Springs Wellness Center. It would be a place of therapy and holistic well-being where compassion, collaboration, and continual growth formed the foundation of our services. This foundational understanding guided every subsequent decision, ensuring that every decision we made during construction was in alignment with the core values of the center.

Securing the perfect location was key. The property had to resonate with the type of energy that welcomed a nurturing environment for our clients. Simultaneously, securing funding required diligence, creativity, and a commitment to our mission. It was about seeking partnerships with like-minded individuals and organizations who shared our vision for holistic wellness.

When it was time to design the interior, every element, from the color scheme to the layout, was chosen with care to foster a sense of tranquility and comfort.

Hiring a team aligned with the center's mission was equally essential. Each member brought their expertise and contributed a strong passion and dedication to their work.

Crafting a marketing campaign to attract our ideal clients was another aspect of bringing our vision to fruition. It was about conveying the essence of Healing Springs our values, our services, and the transformative experiences we offered in a way that spoke directly to the woman who was ready to heal wholeheartedly. We pride ourselves in building a community, both online and offline, where individuals feel seen, heard, and supported on their wellness journey.

Throughout this process, spiritual alignment was infused in every moving part. We surrendered to the flow of the universe, knowing that each step taken was leading us closer to completion. In the end, this blueprint encompassed a bigger picture. Our path was not just about reaching a destination but embracing the challenges, the triumphs, and the lessons we learned along the way. By staying true to our values and our purpose, we were able to uphold our commitment to making a meaningful and lasting impact in the lives of those we serve.

Transitioning to Sandra's Story: Embracing Challenges and Manifesting Success

Sandra's story, as a consultant overcoming procrastination, reflects our commitment to intentional action and mindset transformation. Her tendency to procrastinate stemmed from a deep-seated fear of failure and perfectionism. Through our sessions, she came to understand that these issues were not only hindering her professional development, but negatively affecting her self-perception.

When Sandra first approached me, she was gripped by the fear of failure and perfectionism, which were evidence of a larger struggle with selfworth. She harbored a vision of running a successful consultancy, but allowed the uncertainty of her capabilities to hold her hostage. To address these challenges, we focused on a holistic approach that intertwined faith with small, obtainable goals. Sandra started each day with affirmations and visualization exercises that were ingrained in her spiritual beliefs. These practices reinforced her faith in herself, acted as a daily reminder of her potential, and how she is connected to a higher purpose. Her morning mantra, "I am skilled, I am capable, and I am divinely guided to lead my consultancy with confidence" became her new self-talk that restored her inner voice and solidified her faith when countering any doubts.

Our weekly accountability check-ins monitored Sandra's spiritual and professional growth, and gave her an opportunity to see the divine hand at work in her life. Each small achievement was celebrated as evidence of her trust in God and materializing her vision, which significantly alleviated the pressures she once felt.

As Sandra took steps that were parallel with her spiritual beliefs and professional goals, her consultancy business began to flourish. She defined her brand, launched her website, and started attracting her ideal clients. These milestones and the advancement in Sandra's professional career were confirmations that when she married her spirituality with her daily action steps, she not only achieved her goals but proved that faith, when activated, can be a strong catalyst in helping her to reach unimaginable levels.

Now, it's your turn to craft an intentional action plan that resonates with your goals and aspirations. Below are six steps designed with a sense of purpose and spiritual alignment to guide you to your dreams.

Step 1: Clarify Your Vision

Start by painting a vivid picture of your ultimate vision. What does success look like to you? Is it launching a new business, growing in your career, or achieving personal growth? Write down your vision in detail, allowing yourself to dream big and set the stage for what you're aiming to achieve.

Step 2: Set Achievable Goals

With your vision in mind, break it down into smaller, more manageable goals. These goals should be SMART: Specific, Measurable, Achievable, Relevant, and Timebound. For instance, if your dream involves opening a private practice, one of your goals might be to finalize a business plan within the next six months or to secure funding by a specific date.

Step 3: Outline Actionable Steps

For each of your goals, identify the specific actions needed to achieve them. These should be straightforward tasks such as researching potential locations, networking with industry professionals, or enhancing your skills through targeted training. Assign deadlines to each action to hold yourself accountable and on track.

Step 4: Build Your Support System

Determine who in your circle can provide support and accountability. This could be a mentor, a professional coach, or a group of peers who share similar aspirations. Communicate your goals and plans to them, and set up regular check-ins to discuss your progress, tackle any challenges, and celebrate your achievements.

Step 5: Embrace Hope and Faith

Incorporate the type of activities that nurture your spiritual connection and reinforce your belief in your vision's manifestation. Daily affirmations, prayer, meditation, and journaling can be cathartic in maintaining a positive outlook and staying aligned with your purpose. Have faith and trust in the timing, knowing that everything will unfold as it's meant to.

Step 6: Reflect and Pivot When Necessary

Make it a habit to periodically review your progress. Be open to adjusting your plan as you gain new insights or encounter unexpected obstacles. Celebrate every victory, no matter how small, and learn from any setbacks. Lastly, allow flexibility and resilience to act as safeguards as you move closer to your desired outcome.

Your dreams are within reach. With a clear target in mind, a culture of go-getters by your side, and a heart full of unshakeable faith, you are well on your way to having limitless success. Let this Intentional Action Plan be your guide as you step boldly toward your goals, transforming your vision into the life you've always wanted. Download the Intentional Action Plan at www.shawnielchamanlal.com/resources and feel free to share your first step in the **Unapologetic Success Facebook Group.**

CHAPTER 5

Building Inner Strength

Your beliefs become your thoughts, your thoughts
become your words, your words become your actions,
your actions become your habits, your habits become
your values, your values become your destiny.

— Mahatma Gandhi

Why Cultivating a Worthiness Practice is a Must

Adopting a limitless vision for our lives means we must establish worthiness and fundamentally change how we see ourselves and our place in the world. Improving my self-belief began with a series of shifts in understanding how I approached relationships. A broken engagement in my twenties symbolized a brokenness within me. I entertained a pattern of emotionally unavailable men that left me feeling unloved, unappreciated, and subconsciously unworthy of love.

During childhood, my absentee father left me with unhealed wounds of abandonment. This affected how I saw myself early on and contributed to my unhealthy relationship patterns, causing me to seek validation externally, often in ways that perpetuated emotional manipulation. In search of healing, I turned to therapy and pulled out my journal to uncover and understand my internal beliefs, patterns, and motivations. What I discovered was that I'd been living with a scarcity mindset, one lingering with hurt and pain that came from a history of feeling like I wasn't good enough or deserving of true love.

Through therapy, I started to rewrite my internal narrative. I challenged myself to comprehend how my upbringing and experiences had shaped my outlook on love and the relationships I was in. My father not being in my life had instilled a fear that all men would eventually leave, causing me to unconsciously recreate old traumas and chase after unhealthy relationships that couldn't fill the void. Once I identified this pattern, I began to see my worthiness not as something determined by external validation, but as an intrinsic value I could work on within myself.

Healing required letting go of past hurts and reprogramming my belief system to one that exalted in opportunities and deservingness. Every decision demanded that I set healthy boundaries, practice selfcare, and learn to treat myself with the kindness and compassion I would offer a close friend. Patience and vulnerability were necessary being that this new way of establishing good relationships didn't happen overnight. Gradually, I would meet individuals from a place of fullness rather than lack, and I attracted people who were attracted to my authenticity and complemented the good qualities that I offered.

Kind-hearted, sympathetic, and emotionally present are a few of the qualities I hoped for in a life-long partner and are exactly what I cherish in my husband. Our relationship became a source of joy and growth, confirming that I could break free from the cycle of unsatisfying relationships. I no longer felt confined by the past that no longer served the woman and wife I had become. Instead, I researched what harmonious relationships looked like, drawing inspiration from people who modeled open communication, mutual respect, and trust. It reconditioned my thinking and gave me the assertiveness to affirm, "I deserve a healthy, loving relationship, and I am capable of creating it."

Now, let's put "developing your own worthiness" into practice. I've developed a 4-part framework known as C.A.R.E., designed to propel you through the essential stages of self-improvement, self-acceptance, achievement and fulfillment. You will be able to assess and pinpoint where you are and actively move along to where you want to be. Here's how you can start taking C.A.R.E. of yourself:

- Clarity (C): Begin by dissecting the origins and impacts of your patterns, behaviors, and beliefs. Through self-awareness and possibly therapy, fully grasp how these same habits and attitudes brought you to where you are in your life and formed the relationships you currently have. Identifying the root causes is essential for initiating meaningful change.

- Acknowledgment (A): Recognize and accept your patterns without casting judgment. You want to come from a place of understanding why their presence is in your life and the influence they've had over you. This empowers you to regain control over your thoughts and emotions.

- Reframe (R): Engage in positive affirmations and constructive self-talk to reinforce your inherent worth and capabilities. Confront and replace lingering thoughts of self-doubt with uplifting, positive statements about yourself. This part is specially dedicated to establishing the type of belief system that directly aligns with your short and long-term goals, and true potential.

- Empowerment (E): Empowerment comes from acknowledging your progress and recognizing your potential for further growth. Commit to your personal growth by continuously acquiring new knowledge and skills to bolster your self-esteem and confidence in your ability to achieve your dreams.

How Laura Transformed Doubts Into Success With The C.A.R.E. Framework

When I think of the perfect illustration of how the C.A.R.E. Framework works, I'm reminded of the story of my client Laura. When Laura came to me for therapy, she was at a critical juncture in her life, managing a business that felt stagnant and in a marriage that, while good, did not fully satisfy her needs. She questioned her potential to achieve greater heights of success and to experience a more passionate connection with her spouse.

Through dedicated work within the C.A.R.E. Framework, Laura confronted and dismantled the limiting beliefs that held her back. It started with her bringing clarity to the habits and patterns that brought her and her husband to this stagnant point, and what she actually wanted at this stage of her marriage. She admitted to the part she played in her marriage and together we reframed the thoughts that were preventing her from the agape or highest form of love she longed to feel. She began affirming her strengths and worth, declaring, "I am a powerhouse in my business," and "I deserve a partnership filled with love and mutual respect." Saying these statements daily shifted her life from park to overdrive.

To improve her relationship, both Laura and her husband made the decision to attend couples counseling. This step was aimed at enhancing their relationship skills and improving the intimacy shared between them. The sessions provided techniques and strategies to help them communicate more effectively, giving them a different perspective of each other and restoring their bond. As a result, Laura's marriage evolved into the type of relationship that can be described by laughter, shared dreams, and a renewed love founded on mutual respect and trust.

On a professional level, Laura sharpened her business skills by taking workshops and courses to enhance her communication and leadership strategies. This not only built her business acumen, but now her confidence shines through brighter than ever. With a clearer vision, she propelled her business to new heights, fostering a culture of innovation and excellence that resonated throughout her team. The impact was clear: her business gained recognition, her client base grew, and her revenue increased substantially.

By committing to the work, Laura shifted her mindset from one of scarcity to one of abundance, confirming the belief that she could indeed have it all success and fulfillment. She is proof that changing one's beliefs and engaging in intentional actions can create the life one deserves.

Now, let's turn our attention to you. Reflect on the obstacles that may be blocking your path to success. How might addressing your self-doubt, fears, and unresolved issues open the door to a life filled with achievement and satisfaction? The C.A.R.E. Framework is here to guide you through this process of change, providing a structured method for realizing your dreams and validating your self-worth.

CHAPTER 6

Embrace Your Journey

Turning Criticism Into Opportunities

Confronting our inner critics, those uninvited guests that frequently infiltrate our thoughts and feelings, can take charge during import-ant times of decision-making and action-taking. *Can you really make it to the top, given your past failures? Why put yourself through this again?* Although these voices are part of our innate defense mechanisms, they can also hinder our ability to reach our full potential. This unsettling voice typically sneaks in to "protect us," keeping us safe from disappointment and failure, but often at the cost of us remaining constrained. It acts as a shield against the fears of uncertainty and the discomfort of facing the unknown.

A strategy I've employed is to personify my inner critic, giving it the name "Debbie Downer." Addressing these worrisome thoughts with humor and directness weakens their influence, revitalizes my belief in my own abilities, and reinforces my commitment to my goals. Once again it's a deliberate action to face my doubts and fears head-on. This inner voice is normal, especially when pushing our upper limits, and these feelings are a common thread in the human experience, particularly for women and women leaders facing unique challenges and societal expectations.

Engaging with Debbie Downer is empowering. Taking an active stance against our inner critic allows us to initiate a dialogue, scrutinizing beliefs like *Who says I can't have it all a fulfilling career and a rich personal life?* while reiterating our commitment to our vision for our life. This straightforward-talking strategy diminishes the influence of our doubts and fears and recalibrates our mindset to pursue our goals and dreams with renewed confidence and clarity.

Silencing Debbie Downer is only the first step, because you must understand where these thoughts are coming from so you can reframe them. We should question their truth, origin, and current usefulness. For every doubt or fear, ask yourself "Is this really true?" "Does this belief serve my growth and well-being?"

Take a moment to turn inward and communicate with your inner dialogue. Does your critical voice have a name? Can you visualize its appearance? Reflect on the messages it whispers (or shouts) to you. Often our little cynical voice tends to be the loudest when we're stressed out, perceive threats ahead, or when we are venturing into unfamiliar territory. When you hear the voice creeping in, pay attention to what is going on in your internal and external world. What themes do these messages follow? Are they questioning your abilities or perhaps echoes of past criticisms?

Now it's time to give a name and identity to the voice that counters your inner Debbie Downer. Let's call this voice of optimism "Vicky The Victorious," your cheerleader, your advocate, your reminder of the potential you carry within. Vicky views challenges as opportunities. She reminds you of your past successes, and encourages you to leap even when the outcome is uncertain.

What does Vicky say to you? Perhaps it's words that remind you of your strength, intelligence, and value. Maybe she reminds you of the times you've fallen short of a goal, but didn't give up and your perseverance paid off. Vicky encourages you to embrace change, learn from mistakes, and celebrate every step forward, no matter what.

Although Vicky promotes positive thinking, she actively cultivates a mindset that supports your growth, resilience, and well-being, too. It's knowing that while the Debbie Downer voice may be part of your mental landscape, it doesn't have to control your thoughts or actions. You have the power to choose which voice to amplify.

Whenever Debbie Downer speaks up, invite Vicky The Victorious into the conversation. Let her respond to those negative outlooks, offer a new perspective on your fears, and remind you of your inner strength and accomplishments. This practice is revolutionary, changing the narrative from limitation to limitless potential. Remember, the dialogue between Debbie Downer and Vicky The Victorious reflect your internal world. And by nurturing Vicky, you're not just silencing your critic, you're elevating your spirit, one empowered thought at a time.

Subduing Shadows: From Inner Critic to Inner Champion

My client Brandy is a good example of what happens when you engage with, rather than evade, the inner critic we all wrestle with. She didn't ignore the Debbie Downer antics, but rather wanted to understand, negotiate, and ultimately transform them into stepping stones for her benefit. Here's how Brandy released Debbie Downer's unnerving thoughts to emerge as a courageous woman in leadership.

1. **Acknowledgment of the Inner Critic.** Brandy's first step was to admit that the presence of her inner

critic "Negative Nancy" existed, and that it was not an adversary, but part of her protective mechanism. This acknowledgment reduced the critic's authority over her decisions and self-esteem.

2. **Unraveling the Roots.** She courageously explored the origins of her thoughts, tracing them back to past experiences and what she believed society expected of her as a Black woman in leadership. This exploration shed light on the critic's foundation, making it less intimidating and more manageable.

3. **Reframing the Dialogue.** With a deeper understanding of where her doubts originated, Brandy began the work of reframing these narratives. She questioned the accuracy and helpfulness of her inner critic's messages, paving the way for a more positive self-perception.

4. **Fostering Positive Self-Talk.** Brandy cultivated an empowering inner dialogue that celebrated her strengths, past successes, and the unique perspective she brought to her role. This positive

self-talk was instrumental in bringing her focus from limitations to possibilities.

5. **Commitment to Growth.** Admitting that there were areas for improvement, Brandy dedicated herself to personal and professional development, seeking out resources and mentorship to take her skills up a notch and become fearless.

By acknowledging, understanding, reframing, and actively developing a positive self-dialogue, she boldly stepped into her role as a newly appointed superintendent, and was now in position to redefine leadership for women in her field.

Brandy's narrative is a reminder that our inner critics, coupled with insight and purpose, can transform from barriers to catalysts for personal and professional growth. If you're willing to courageously face bad habits like procrastination or seeking the approval of others, then this task is accessible to you. As you reflect on your own journey, consider the steps Brandy took and how you might apply them to where you are. Tap into your emotions, dialogue with your doubts, and don't forget that every critic, internal or external, can become a champion in your corner.

Now, I encourage you to make the decision to identify your inner critic, give it a name, and begin the process of transforming it from a source of not enough to a wellspring overflowing with strength and positive affirmations. Share your experience, your struggles, and your victories with a community that supports and uplifts you such as the **Unapologetic Success Facebook Group**. Together, let's turn our inner critics into our most powerful allies on the path to achieving our dreams.

CHAPTER 7

Unstoppable, Unshakable Confidence

"Imagine striding through life with the unshakeable confidence of Serena Williams on the tennis court or Beyoncé on the stage this is the world we're claiming." – Shawniel Chamanlal

The Essence of Inner Strength

Why do you want more? Starting Healing Springs Wellness Center was a dream met with skepticism by some. Many would question my why, mistaking my ambition for greed or my expansive vision for vanity. It was an awakening that your belief in fulfilling your dreams is often met with the disbelief of others. But if there's one thing my mom, Beyoncé, and Serena taught me, it's that confidence is the compass that guides you through the fog of naysayers. It's about setting boundaries around your dreams, shielding them from the projections of those who have yet to find their own light.

Unstoppable, Unshakable Confidence is a movement about owning your space and expanding on it, while inviting others to rise to the top with you. It's a legacy passed down from the women who have gone on before us, a torch we carry forward for the generations to come. It's knowing that, in a world eager to dim our light, we choose to shine brighter, inspiring others to ignite their own inner flame. For every woman walking the path from uncertainty to confidence, your journey is not just about reaching a destination, but inspiring others to say yes to starting their own.

Unleashing Potential: Harnessing Inner Strength Through Inspirational Stories

Initially overshadowed by self-doubt and whispers of inadequacy, my client, Anna discovered the magic in her alter ego, blossoming from a wallflower into an outgoing high achiever. Much like the iconic Beyoncé channels Sasha Fierce for an extra boost of boldness on stage, Anna knew she needed to summon her own vibrant, fearless version ready to conquer her performance in the field.

Inspired by successful figures, Anna recognized that active confidence is far more impactful than passive contemplation. She began to visualize herself as a dynamic powerhouse, capable of commanding any room or situation with poise and authority. She imagined future successes, but not before recalling past victories of both major accomplishments (and minor ones), that reaffirmed her competence and resilience.

Furthermore, Anna, like the female leaders I've mentioned before, adopted the practice of speaking life through affirmations. Understanding that words wield immense power, she began a daily ritual of positive self-talk, reinforcing her strengths, value, and skillset. This mirrored the behaviors of renowned figures like Michelle Obama and Shonda Rhimes, who both speak publicly about the role that self-belief and positive affirmation has played in their lives. Michelle Obama, with her poised and grounded presence, often discusses how affirmations helped her navigate the pressures of being First Lady, while Shonda Rhimes, creator of groundbreaking TV shows, shares how by asserting her aspirations, her career became unrecognizable.

Anna's newfound confidence and inner strength became a core part of her identity, and it changed how she interacted with the world. Her story reminds us that confidence can be consciously built through a blend of self-reflection, positive reinforcement, and a steadfast commitment to personal goals.

For women in leadership, Anna serves as an example of how you can elevate to new levels when you nurture an inner sanctuary of self-assurance, particularly in environments that frequently test our worth and competence. Drawing inspiration from trailblazers like Obama and Rhimes who have both faced and overcome considerable obstacles helps solidify our own narratives of success. By embracing their resilience and reinforcing our personal journeys of growth, we can develop a confidence that is not only robust, but also an unstoppable force driving us toward our highest aspirations.

The title of this chapter is "Unstoppable, Unshakable Confidence," a mantra, a way of life that you're invited to add to your personal development. It's about embracing the fullness of who you are, recognizing your inherent worth, and stepping boldly into the world with the conviction that you are capable, deserving, and ready to claim your place. Let's carry this torch of confidence, passing it on to every woman we encounter, lighting the way for a future where their inner strength and pride is as unshakeable as the earth beneath our feet.

Importance of a Positive Environment: Your surroundings can significantly influence your mental state and energy levels, and it's essential to create an environment that fosters positivity and resilience. By choosing to immerse yourself in uplifting and motivational content, you ensure that your community is primed for growth and positivity. This can help maintain your momentum even when struggles appear, providing a steady stream of inspiration that keeps you focused on your goals.

Impact of Inspirational Media: Surrounding yourself with music that moves you, participating in inspirational talks, and absorbing the wisdom of trailblazers reinforce your mindset with the belief that anything is possible. Soul-stirring music and motivational speeches can dramatically shift your emotional and psychological state. Music, for instance, has the ability to energize, soothe, and inspire, while the right words at the right time can transform your perspective and encourage you to persist. These elements can turn your doubts into determination and your fears into fortitude.

Learning from Trailblazers: The stories and wisdom of those who have paved the way in any field offer invaluable nuggets that teach us lessons about bouncing back, creating a master plan, and what success can look like. By studying trailblazers, you not only avoid common pitfalls, but also gain insights into effective tactics and mental frameworks that can propel you forward. These stories remind you that every journey has its obstacles, and they equip you with the strategies to overcome your own.

Building Unshakeable Confidence: When you regularly consume content that reinforces your capacity to succeed, you begin to internalize these messages. This continuous reinforcement takes your self-esteem up a notch and secures your belief in your ability to do whatever you put your mind to. You become immovable, making you more resilient against negativity and doubt.

Unlocking the Doors to Your Dreams: Maintaining a feel-good attitude keeps your mental space clear of negativity, and when you're filled with affirmative and motivational influences, you unlock the doors to your future. You stimulate mental pathways that lead to creativity, opportunity, and proactive versus reactive behaviors. Each step taken in this enriched environment brings you closer to your personal and professional aspirations, enabling you to step into your greatness with conviction and poise.

Ultimately, these keys help you to cope with the present and crack the code to thrive in the future. They ensure that your journey is not only successful, but also sustainable and fulfilling, enabling you to live out your greatness with confidence and joy.

I've created the Unstoppable, Unshakeable Confidence Worksheet to help you pinpoint the qualities you admire in others and to see how you can embody them in your own life. Download your guide at www.shawniel-chamanlal.com/resources.

CHAPTER 8

The Heart of Fulfillment

Why Gratitude is The Pathway to Joyful Success

In the hustle of achieving and striving, it's easy to overlook the power of gratitude. Yet, it's your ability to give thanks that can make our success journey filled with joy and fulfillment. Grounding ourselves in gratitude means shifting our focus from what we're chasing to what we already have, from what's missing to the abundance that surrounds us. This attitude prepares a space from which all of our desires can manifest more effortlessly.

Abraham Hicks, a notable figure in the world of spiritual teaching, emphasizes the profound impact our thoughts and emotions have on our reality. Their teachings on the law of attraction highlight gratitude as a key component in aligning ourselves with the universe's abundant energy. It's in this form of alignment that enables us to draw closer to our deepest desires.

Gratitude does more than just make us feel better. It actively changes our energy from a state of lack to one of more than enough. This vibrational vortex overpowers the resistance that often stands between us and our goals, turning our vibration into a magnet that attracts experiences, people, and opportunities that resonate with our desires.

Icons like Oprah Winfrey have long championed the transformative power of gratitude. Oprah's practice of listing five things she's grateful for each night is a testament to how gratitude can center us, offering stability and perspective amidst the fluctuations of life. This practice of acknowledging our blessings, big or small, fosters a sense of contentment and joy that fuels our path to success.

Anchoring Success: How Joan's Journey of Gratitude Enhances Life's Richness

Joan's story showcases how gratitude can fundamentally anchor us in our achievements, providing a barrier against the fears that often accompany success. When Joan embraced the practice of staying present and grateful, she discovered that this mindset was crucial for safeguarding her joy and the fruits of her labor. Her story teaches us that our achievements are not ephemeral, but are significant milestones that should be celebrated and cherished.

The role of self-awareness in this process cannot be overstated. It enables us to identify and counteract the fears and negative thoughts that can cloud our perception of our accomplishments. Joan journaled, meditated, and practiced mindfulness, and each stimulated an inner dialogue that anchored her in the present. These practices reminded her of her resilience and the tangible nature of her achievements.

Why is this internal work so essential? It ensures that we savor our current successes without being in constant pursuit of the next milestone. It builds a sense of security around our achievements, recognizing them as manifestations of our dedication and resilience. This solid foundation of gratitude and mindfulness prepares us to face challenges and setbacks with poise, continually reinforcing our confidence in our abilities to achieve and relish in success.

Gratitude effectively shifts our perspective from one of scarcity to one of abundance, from worrying to overflowing with joy. This is why I recommend integrating a gratitude journal into your daily routine to enrich your life. The easy habit of recording things that you're thankful for can significantly enhance your mental well-being, relationships, and overall happiness. Acknowledging our blessings amplifies the beauty and abundance of our lives. It's a reminder of the wealth that surrounds us, even during challenging times, while giving the abundance that is already present in your life, permission to further bring you joy, success, and fulfillment.

To cultivate this mindset, start by incorporating specific gratitude journal prompts into your writing. The following prompts are designed to focus your attention not on what you lack, but on the abundance that surrounds you.

1. **What are three things you are grateful for today?**

   Reflect on both the small joys and significant achievements of your day to get the full spectrum of positivity in your life.

2. **Who made a positive difference in your day and how?**

   Think about the actions of others, which helps to appreciate good relationships and deepen those connections.

3. **What challenge did you overcome today that you're thankful for?**

   Identify the lessons learned from your daily challenges, and make a note of how they contribute to your personal growth.

4. **What lesson did you learn recently that you're grateful for?**

Contemplate the insights gained from recent experiences and allow your takeaways to foster a mindset of continuous learning and growth.

5. **What's a simple pleasure that brought you joy today?**

Notice everyday comforts and instances that make you smile to enhance gratitude for the present moment.

Share your gratitude and the insights you gain with the **Unapologetic Success Facebook Group**. Together, let's cultivate an attitude of gratitude, because after all, the destination of your dreams is best when you appreciate every step along the way.

CHAPTER 9

Celebrate Your Wins

"Let every victory, no matter its size, be a testament to
your journey's brilliance."

– Shawniel Chamanlal

The Building Blocks for Lasting Success

I n the complex fabric of our lives, each success,
whether monumental or modest, adds a unique
texture that adds color to our entire narrative.
Celebrating these achievements is not merely about
recognizing effort. It is a crucial practice that bolsters
our self-belief and lays a solid foundation for future
successes. This method, grounded in academic research
and enriched by practical experience, highlights the

importance of positive reinforcement in fostering both personal and professional growth.

Looking back over my life, there were several times I failed to hit pause and appreciate everything I had accomplished. I was always fixated on the next challenge or task to check off my to-do list. However, it is precisely in celebrating our achievements that we find the strength for future endeavors. This act of celebrating yourself serves as inspiration to those who are watching us and puts us in position of becoming mentors and exemplars of what is achievable.

In fact, it was a mentor, who once guided me, who brought this to my attention. This mentor reached out to express admiration for the path I had forged, significantly impacting me and reminding me of the dreams that were no longer imaginations but were now my life. Such moments of recognition rejuvenate our spirits and remind us of the obstacles we have surmounted, affirming:

"I am the realization of my ancestors' wildest dreams." "I embody success in every aspect of my life."

"I am surrounded by abundance."

Celebrating Milestones: The Power of Acknowledging Every Victory

Developing a habit of regular reflection on your journey, celebrating every victory, and learning from setbacks keeps you connected to your true purpose. Personally, making it a routine to journal about my weekly victories has deepened my gratitude and reinforced my belief in life's abundance. This ritual of acknowledgment keeps us grounded in the present, enhancing our appreciation for the path we've traveled.

I urge you to make time in your daily or weekly schedule to acknowledge your achievements and assess how this assignment affects your well-being. Do you feel an upsurge of excitement? A greater sense of pride? More fulfillment? Appreciate these feelings for they are the force that moves us down the yellow brick road.

Reward Yourself. It's essential to honor your hard work with rewards that resonate with your soul. Following the launch of my wellness center, I treated myself to weekly spa visits, acknowledging the effort and passion that brought my vision to life. Identify what truly brings you joy and allow it to be a reward for your dedication.

Share Your Wins. Contrary to the belief that we should minimize our achievements, we must share and celebrate them, especially with those who support us.

In the Unapologetic Success Community, we commit to fostering a space where victories are praised collectively, reinforcing the value of perseverance and hard work.

Sheryl Sandberg's Paradigm of Celebration

Sheryl Sandberg, the COO of Facebook and author of *Lean In*, has been a force in the corporate world, not only breaking glass ceilings, but also fervently championing women's empowerment. Her holistic approach to celebrating achievements incorporates personal reflection, public acknowledgment, and promoting a supportive community that rejoices in one's accomplishments and values success.

Personal Reflection and Goal Setting. Sandberg emphasizes the importance of personal reflection in recognizing one's achievements. She advocates for setting specific, measurable goals as benchmarks for success, ensuring that each milestone, no matter the size, is announced and commended. Goal-setting and taking time to think about what you've been able to accomplish allows women in leadership to see their perseverance and tangible results of their hard work. There's a paradigm from viewing success as a distant, almost unattainable goal, to seeing it as a series of achievable steps, each worthy of recognition and celebration.

Public Acknowledgment. Sandberg also champions the idea of vocalizing achievements, not as an act of boasting, but as a celebration of your hard work, resilience, and determination. By openly sharing her own successes and challenges, she encourages other women to take pride in their accomplishments. This public acknowledgment serves as a powerful counter-narrative to the societal expectation that women should remain modest about their achievements. It sends a clear message that success is not something to be whispered about, but spoken loudly and proudly.

Creating a Supportive Community. Through initiatives like LeanIn.org and the concept of "Lean In Circles," Sandberg fosters a community of support for women to join forces and celebrate their wins together. These circles provide a safe space for women to share their achievements, learn from each other's experiences, and offer mutual support. This community amplifies the impact of individual successes, creating a ripple effect that inspires and empowers other women to strive for their own goals.

The positive effects of celebrating wins, as advocated by Sandberg, extend far beyond individual achievement. They foster a culture of empowerment, where women are encouraged to aim high, recognize their worth, and support one another in their pursuits. This changes the narrative around women's success, moving from a space of competition and comparison to one of collaboration and celebration.

In a world where women's achievements are often overshadowed or downplayed, Sandberg's story and her advocacy for celebrating wins stand as a beacon of change. It challenges the status quo and encourages women to own their success, celebrate it without apology, and use it as a platform to uplift others. This approach not only enhances our own lives, but shatters societal paradigms, paving the way for a future where women's achievements are recognized, celebrated, and used as a source of inspiration for generations to come.

As we conclude this chapter, let us fully embrace the thought of celebrating our wins with open hearts. There is infinite potential within us ready to manifest in all its glory, and we must understand that reflecting on our growth refuels our confidence, elevates our vibration, and places us in a state of being unstoppable.

So, take a moment to honor your life's journey, join our community, and let's raise a toast to every step of our collective efforts toward unapologetic success. Here's to tossing confetti for each win, the very building blocks of a life marked by lasting success and boundless joy.

Closing

You've now turned to the final page of this book, but let's be clear, this isn't the end. You're at the beginning of something extraordinary. Imagine standing in front of a door, beyond which lies everything you've ever dreamed of abundance, desire, worthiness, growth, confidence, courage, gratitude, joy, and unapologetic success. You're about to put the key in the lock, turn it, and walk into an exciting new life where your wildest dreams can now be your reality.

Throughout these pages, you've been trained and equipped with the tools, insights, and inspirations to craft a life of limitless possibilities. You've learned to paint your desires in the boldest colors and to stand firm in your worthiness, even when the world tries to shake your confidence. You've discovered the power of gratitude, the joy of the journey, and the importance of celebrating every win, big or small.

This book has been more than just words on a page. You've experienced a glimpse of what it means to live without ceilings, to believe deeply in the abundance that surrounds you, and to pursue your dreams with relentless passion. Your heart now resonates with the narrative that "You can have it all!" and live every day as a testament to that truth.

Your life is a masterpiece in the making, a canvas where each waking moment adds another stroke of genius, another splash of hue. You stand at the horizon of your future, not as a question mark, but as an exclamation point a bold declaration of your journey, your achievements, and the endless possibilities that await.

Now, as you stand before that door, key in hand, remember what you've learned:

1. **Dreaming Beyond Boundaries:** Dare to dream without limits. Harness the power of scripting and visualization to breathe life into those dreams.

2. **Navigating Success Together:** Surround yourself with uplifters and mentors. Draw strength Unapologetic Success from stories of success that echo your aspirations.

3. **Living Your Truth:** Live life on your terms, pursuing a path that satisfies both your professional ambitions and personal yearnings.

4. **From Vision to Reality:** Navigate through self-doubt to find your strength, turning every obstacle into a milestone on your path to greatness.

6. **Building Inner Strength:** Convert your inner critics into engines of growth, embarking on a journey of self-discovery and empowerment.

7. **Unstoppable, Unshakeable Confidence:** Embody the type of confidence that illuminates the world, facing fears with valor and claiming your space with grace.

8. **The Heart of Fulfillment:** Embrace gratitude as a transformative tool, shifting your focus from scarcity to abundance and aligning yourself with positive energy.

9. **Celebrate Your Wins:** Recognize and revel in every success, nurturing a spirit of celebration and gratitude for your journey and achievements.

What lies ahead is a unique path of action, a call to embrace the new with courage and anticipation. It's an invitation to elevate your mindset with urgency, transforming your future dreams into your present reality.

So, turn the key. Open the door. Cross the threshold. Your dreams are waiting for you with open arms.

About the Author

S hawniel Chamanlal embodies the transformative power of therapy in the entrepreneurial journey. With over 15 years of experience as a licensed clinical social worker, Shawniel has devoted her life to unraveling the complex psychology behind human behavior, with a particular emphasis on the challenges and triumphs faced by women in leadership roles.

Shawniel's road to success was fraught with personal challenges, including navigating failed relationships and the conventional constraints of social work. Her extensive training through mental health counseling and holistic practices has allowed her to heal from within, igniting a passion for assisting others in achieving their dreams.

Her story illustrates resilience, belief, and the relentless pursuit of joy in both personal and professional domains. As the founder and CEO of Healing Springs Wellness Center, Shawniel has not only positioned herself as a leader and innovator in the wellness industry, but has established a sanctuary of support and inclusivity in mental healthcare. Her narrative powerfully demonstrates how grand dreams can be realized when paired with conviction and self-belief.

Driven by the conviction that each of us harbors incredible potential, Shawniel's story serves as a powerful call to those eager to break free from limitations and transform their practices or businesses into thriving, sustainable ventures. Her life, characterized by tales of overcoming trauma, pursuing dreams, and crafting a balanced, fulfilling existence, serves as inspiration for many, and she invites you to start your journey of healing, growth to achieve unmatched success.